AUTOMATED TRADING STRATEGIES
USING C# & NINJATRADER 7
STOCKS | FUTURES | FOREX

RYAN MOORE

Automated Trading Strategies using C# and NinjaTrader 7

An introduction for .NET developers

Ryan Moore

Tweet This Book!

Please help Ryan Moore by spreading the word about this book on Twitter!

The suggested hashtag for this book is #csharpninjatrading.

Find out what other people are saying about the book by clicking on this link to search for this hashtag on Twitter:

https://twitter.com/search?q=#csharpninjatrading

Forum

Visit the book's official Discussion Group at http://www.strategyminer.net/forum/

Video Course

For a video walkthrough of the content of this e-book, be sure to try the Udemy Course. If you've purchased the e-book, your purchase price can be applied to the video price - please email ryan@mooretech.us for a coupon code.

Need more help?

Need more help getting up and running with NinjaTrader development? Visit the Strategy Miner website for more information on personalized consulting services.

http://strategyminer.net/

Legal

Trading in any financial market involves substantial risk of loss and is not suitable for all investors. Any style of trading in any market condition is extremely risky and can result in substantial financial losses in a very short period of time . All content provided is for information purposes only and is not intended to be investment advice.

Contents

Prerequisites

System

- Windows XP SP3 or higher
- 2GB RAM+
- Microsoft .NET Framework 3.5+

Software

- Visual Studio .NET 2012 or 2013 (for Visual Studio Debugging as covered in Chapter 6
- NinjaTrader 7 Demo (installation covered in Chapter 1)

Experience

- At minimum, a basic level of C# experience is required. I will provide 3rd party resources for learning C# basics if you're not familiar.
- No trading experience is required, but strongly recommended.

Chapter 1 : Introduction

Introduction

Welcome to Automated Trading Strategies using C# and NinjaTrader 7. In this book, we'll be walking hands-on-tutorial-style through the creation of an automated stock trading strategy using C# and the NinjaTrader platform, as well as methods for testing out its potential success. By the end of this book, you should be able to not only create a simple trading strategy, but also understand how to test it against historical market data, debug it, and even log data into a custom database for further analysis. Even if you have limited C# and trading strategy experience, the examples in this book will provide a great foundation for getting into automated trading and safely testing out strategy ideas before risking real money in the market.

What exactly is Automated Trading?

Automated trading - also referred to as "algorithmic trading" and "black box trading" - could have different definitions depending on the context, but in this book, will refer to a trading strategy as logic implemented in code that can be set up to be executed against historical data (called "back-testing"), or run in the live market to risk real money. This strategy will follow the strict rules defined to determine when to buy and sell investments without human intervention, which hopefully result in a net profit over time.

One great feature of automated trading is that it provides a means for taking the "emotion" out of trading. By specifying concrete rules that are executed by a trading platform (NinjaTrader), you can dismiss the idea constantly monitoring your brokerage account waiting for the perfect moment to execute a trade and then sweating profusely, debating when to make an exit. Instead, you can rest assured that the well-tested logic you have defined will be followed to the letter, executed on the minute, and all without your constant monitoring.

Automated / black box trading has been around for a long time, emerging as early as the 1970s. In recent years however, automated trading has taken over the lion's share of trades executed on major markets, with estimates indicating that over 80% of trades are automatically executed by an algorithm of some sort, rather than manually by a human. Much of this traffic is from large funds, but there is also an increase in small companies and individual traders participating in the automated market.

Because of the well defined rules and the large volume of automated trading, the markets as a whole function much differently than they have in the past. For better or for worse, the markets are now more susceptible to large fluctuations due to simultaneously executed trading strategy executions (such as the 2010 Flash Crash[1]) - but fortunately at other times still functions in a predicable manner.

Not just Stocks

Although we'll refer to "stocks" as the instruments traded by automated strategies, in no way are automated strategies limited to only stocks. NinjaTrader, for example, can be executed on many different investment types, including Stocks, Forex and Futures. In this book, we'll limit our examples to Stock testing, but keep in mind that NinjaTrader can execute strategies against other types of investments, and in any example, a Forex pair or Future contract can be used interchangeably.

Enter NinjaTrader

Although there are numerous platforms that can be used to create automated trading strategies - each with distinct advantages and disadvantages - one of the best (and nearly the only) platforms for strategy development using C# is NinjaTrader. NinjaTrader 7 has been available since 2009, and a new version is rumored to be nearing release. NinjaTrader calls its C# development language *NinjaScript*, it has the same syntax as C#, and can even be debugged using Visual Studio (see chapter 6).

Along with providing a platform for .NET strategy development, back-testing, and execution, NinjaTrader also has a full-featured trading platform feature set, including:

- **Manual Order Entry**: A trader can watch charts and monitor the market before executing a trade manually.
- **Advanced Charting Capabilities**: Chart till you drop! Anything stock data you can imagine can be charted and analyzed in real-time using NinjaTrader.
- **Market Analytics**: Rank and sort instruments in real-time to help make intelligent decisions on your manual trades.

A guided tour of the NinjaTrader platform is available at: http://www.ninjatrader.com/tour.php#[2].

Installing NinjaTrader

To get started with NinjaTrader and C# strategy development, first download the free version of NinjaTrader from the registration page[3].

---

[1]http://en.wikipedia.org/wiki/2010_Flash_Crash

[2]http://www.ninjatrader.com/tour.php

[3]http://www.ninjatrader.com/download-free.php

NinjaTrader's Free Version is an unlimited use download (no expiration on the trial) for Charting, Market Analytics, Trade Simulation, Backtesting and Strategy Development. The Free Version can run while connected to live market data and free 30 day market data trials are available for Futures, Forex and Equities through supported NinjaTrader Brokerage services. In addition, one can subscribe for live market data from Kinetick[4] for affordable, professional data for use with NinjaTrader's Free Version for as long as you like.

After downloading, just complete the NinjaTrader installation and fire it up.

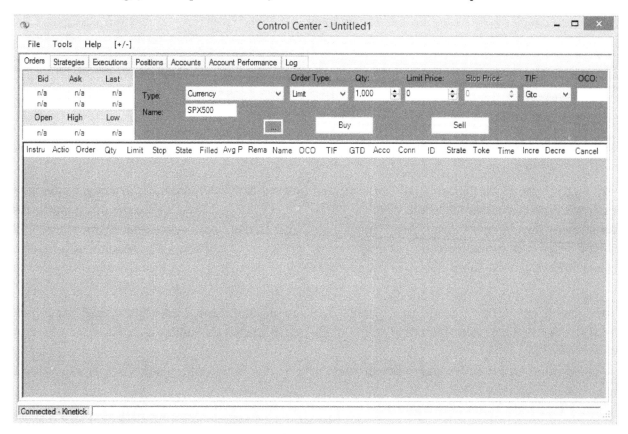

Image 'NinjaTrader 7 UI'

Summary

In this chapter, we've reviewed the very basics of what automated trading is, described NinjaTrader and NinjaScript a bit, and gotten NinjaTrader downloaded and installed. In the next chapter, we'll move on to the basics of NinjaTrader Strategy creation, and prepare to write our first trading strategy.

---

[4]http://www.kinetick.com

Chapter 2 : Creating a Strategy

Introduction

In the first chapter, we covered very basic overview of automated trading and introduced Ninja-Trader, the platform we'll be using for automated trading in this book. As mentioned, NinjaTrader has many capabilities in addition to trading strategy creation and back-testing, but in this book, we'll be primarily focusing on the skills needed to turn trading strategy ideas into reality. In this chapter, we're going to get started creating our first strategy in NinjaScript.

Indicators vs Strategies

As we move forward in NinjaTrader, you'll see a fork in the road between creating Strategies and Indicators, so I'd like to make sure that we understand the difference between a Strategy and an Indicator for those not experienced in automated trading. Both Strategies and Indicators can be developed in NinjaScript (C#), but each performs very different functions:

- **Indicator**: According to Investopedia[5], Indicators are "Statistics used to measure current conditions as well as forecast financial or economic trends". Often, custom Indicators are developed for use in charts, but they can also be used as reference data in custom Strategies - the same as any other measure. Often, we create custom Indicator logic within Strategies as part of the strategy logic.
- **Strategy**: A strategy - also commonly referred to as a trading system - is a collection of logic that may use many (or no) indicators to determine when to buy and when to sell some investment. A strategy can typically be run against historical data (back-tested) or run against live data to execute real-time trades.

There are many many indicators packaged with NinjaTrader out of the box (we'll be using one shortly) and many custom indicators available for purchase on-line. We'll be walking through Strategy creation which could theoretically use any Indicator to perform buys and sells.

Components of an Automated Trading Strategy

Before we create our first strategy code, let's quickly review the components of a typical strategy. Trading strategies can encompass many different types of logic, but generally, they define rules for the following:

---

[5]http://www.investopedia.com/

- **Order Entry Logic** - Logic that defines when a position is entered. This is the most basic and essential of the strategy components.
- **Order Exit Logic** - Logic that defines when positions are exited. Examples include simple profit targets and stop losses.
- **Position Sizing / Account Management** - When entering a position, determines the number of shares to buy. For example, this logic may keep you from ever entering into a position with more than 20% of your total account balance.

In the example strategies we create in this book, we'll be exclusively covering Order Entry and Exit logic - position sizing and account management is a little more tricky when doing historical backtesting, and therefore will be considered outside the scope of this book.

Creating a New NinjaScript Strategy

Now that we understand the difference between a Strategy and an Indicator and have some background on typical strategy components, let's get to business and start creating our first Strategy in NinjaTrader. Although NinjaTrader does provide custom strategy creating using a "Wizard", we're going to strictly focus on fully code-based development. This development kicks off within the NinjaTrader GUI, which we'll walk through in the following steps:

1. Go to the Tools ⇒ New NinjaScript ⇒ Strategy menu to launch the New Strategy Wizard.

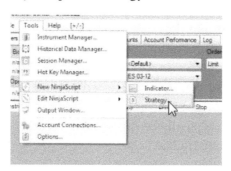

Image 'Creating a New Strategy'

2. Give your strategy a name (I'm calling mine DemoCrossoverStrategy) and a Description. Leave "Calculate on bar close" selected.

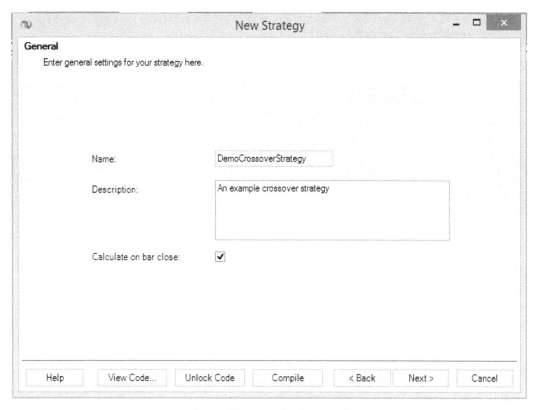

Image 'Naming the Strategy'

3. As shown in the above screen shot, click "Unlock Code" to essentially exit the Strategy Wizard and enter C# Mode.

```
15   // This namespace holds all strategies and is required. Do not change it
16   namespace NinjaTrader.Strategy
17   {
18       /// <summary>
19       /// An example crossover strategy
20       /// </summary>
21       [Description("An example crossover strategy")]
22       public class DemoCrossoverStrategy : Strategy
23       {
24           #region Variables
25           // Wizard generated variables
26           private int myInput0 = 1; // Default setting for MyInput0
27           // User defined variables (add any user defined variables below)
28           #endregion
29
30           /// <summary>
31           /// This method is used to configure the strategy and is called
32           /// </summary>
33           protected override void Initialize()
34           {
35               CalculateOnBarClose = true;
36           }
37
38           /// <summary>
39           /// Called on each bar update event (incoming tick)
40           /// </summary>
41           protected override void OnBarUpdate()
42           {
43           }
44
45           #region Properties
46           [Description("")]
47           [GridCategory("Parameters")]
48           public int MyInput0
49           {
50               get { return myInput0; }
51               set { myInput0 = Math.Max(1, value); }
52           }
53           #endregion
54       }
55   }
```

Image 'Unlocking Strategy Code'

You'll see that when you click "Unlock Code", you are prompted to confirm - say yes, and now there's no going back to "Wizard Mode". After this prompt, NinjaTrader will generate a C# strategy template for you - quick and easy!

NinjaScript Editor

Your new strategy will be opened in the "NinjaScript Editor" which is a very lightweight editor used to create and compile NinjaScripts. In the examples in the rest of this book, we'll be doing C# development within the NinjaScript Editor - you'll find that it has many of the same features as Visual Studio such as auto complete and syntax highlighting.

Here are a few notes on the class you've just generated:

- **CalculateOnBarClose**: This property won't come into play while we're doing historical back-testing. If you are doing advanced development and want to do intra-bar calculations, see the notes here[6] for a better explanation of what this value does.
- **OnBarUpdate**: Here's the entry point to our strategy. This method is executed on every Bar and is where we'll be putting our strategy's logic in the next chapter.
- **MyInput0**: It's a property with a backing field - why would we need this? As we'll see in chapter 5, creating public properties allows us to expose parameters that can be set in the NinjaTrader back-testing UI.

Strategy File Location

The NinjaScript Editor doesn't exactly tell you where your new file was saved to like you may be used to in Visual Studio (or any other editor). To find your new .cs file, take a look in: [your 'documents' folder]NinjaTrader 7\binCustomStrategy.

Summary

Great, we now have a NinjaScript strategy (but with no logic)! In chapter 3, we'll start adding logic to our strategy, and in chapter 4 & chapter 5, we'll compile and back-test the strategy against real historical data.

---

[6]http://www.ninjatrader.com/support/helpGuides/nt7/index.html?calculateonbarclose.htm

Chapter 3 : Strategy Implementation

Introduction

In the previous two chapters, we've set the stage for custom strategy development in C#, learning a bit about strategy development and utilizing the NinjaTrader GUI to auto-generate our first strategy template. In this chapter, we'll get into the nitty-gritty of strategy development by implementing a strategy idea in NinjaScript (C#) code.

Understanding OnBarUpdate

In the strategy we auto-generated in chapter 2, I pointed out the `OnBarUpdate` method that is auto-generated in your new strategy class. This overridable method is called on every bar so your strategy can decide whether it will enter or exit any positions during that bar. But before we get too far... some developers may not be familiar with the term "bar":

What is a bar?

Here is the Investopedia definition of "Bar"[a]. In the context of NinjaTrader, a Bar can be thought of as the unit of time measurement that we are using for our trading strategy. For example, if we are using daily bars (as we will be in this book), then each bar will be composed of all of the data contained within a day of trading (low, high, open, close, etc). In NinjaTrader Bar data could go all the way down to 1 minute, and of course in High Frequency trading, typically goes down to the millisecond.

[a]http://www.investopedia.com/terms/b/bar.asp

As mentioned, our `OnBarUpdate` method is where we'll be placing our strategy's logic. This logic will be evaluated every "interval" during active trading days. So, if we're working with 1 hour intervals, or bars, this method will be called every hour to give us a hook to implement our logic.

Other NinjaScript Overridable Methods

Along with the exceptionally useful `OnBarUpdate` method, NinjaTrader provides numerous other overridable methods on the Strategy class which get fired during different events in a Strategy's lifecycle. Understanding and reacting to these methods is essential for good strategy development. Some of these methods include:

- OnConnectionStatus[7]: Called when the connection status of your data feed changes. For example, if your machine loses internet connectivity and the data feed connection is lost, you can handle the scenario in this method.
- OnFundamentalData[8]: Called for every change in fundamental data for the underlying instrument. Not operational in backtesting, so we won't focus on it in this book.
- OnOrderUpdate[9]: Called when an order managed by your strategy changes state. This method is essential for live-market strategy execution, as it contains information about the actual order that was placed (or not placed) when you've tried to enter into a position.
- OnStartUp[10]: Fires when a strategy is initialized (similar to the `Initialize` method). In some cases it is better to use this than the `Initialize` method for variable initialization.
- OnTermination[11]: Called when a strategy's session is complete and the strategy class is being terminated. We'll utilize this method in the database connectivity example in Chapter 8.

Golden Cross Strategy

Let's kick off our strategy development by sketching out some pseudo-code for a basic strategy. As a demo, let's try to implement common "Golden Cross" strategy as described in this article[12]. First, I'll pseudo-code it out:

```
IF the simple moving average (SMA) of the investment in
a 10 period timespan just moved up and crossed over the
simple moving average (SMA) of the 20 period timespan
        THEN
        BUY the investment. Set a stop-loss at 10% loss and a profit target at 20\
% gain.
```

> **Note** If you're not familiar with Simple Moving Average (SMA), please check out this Investopedia article[a] which defines it as:
>
> ───────────
> [a]http://www.investopedia.com/terms/s/sma.asp

---

[7]http://www.ninjatrader.com/support/helpGuides/nt7/onconnectionstatus.htm

[8]http://www.ninjatrader.com/support/helpGuides/nt7/onfundamentaldata.htm

[9]http://www.ninjatrader.com/support/helpGuides/nt7/onorderupdate.htm

[10]http://www.ninjatrader.com/support/helpGuides/nt7/onstartup.htm

[11]http://www.ninjatrader.com/support/helpGuides/nt7/ontermination.htm

[12]http://etfdb.com/etf-education/3-simple-moving-average-etf-trading-strategies/

> *A simple, or arithmetic, moving average that is calculated by adding the closing price of the security for a number of time periods and then dividing this total by the number of time periods.*

The pseudo-code looks relatively easy, right? Let's make the jump into C# in the NinjaScript Editor and translate that logic into code! If you hit the "Unlock Code" button in the previous chapter, the editor should have opened with the default strategy template. Listed below is the C# implementation of our pseudo-code, which we'll dissect:

Golden Cross Strategy in C#

```
1   protected override void Initialize()
2   {
3       CalculateOnBarClose = true;
4
5           // we'll set the stop loss for our positions globally
6           SetStopLoss(CalculationMode.Percent, .1);
7             SetProfitTarget(CalculationMode.Percent, .2);
8   }
9
10  /// <summary>
11  /// Called on each bar update event (incoming tick)
12  /// </summary>
13  protected override void OnBarUpdate()
14  {
15          var sma1 = SMA(10);
16          var sma2 = SMA(20);
17
18          if (CrossAbove(sma1, sma2, 1)) {
19                  EnterLong();
20          }
21  }
```

Get the Code *Here's the link[13] to the full strategy class we've created for reference.*

C# Reference

As mentioned previously, we're not going to get into any C# language specific details in this book since there are already many excellent publications information available. For a good kick-start in

---

C# development, I'd recommend Pro C# 5.0 and the .NET 4.5 Framework[a] which provides a wealth of C# knowledge.

[a]http://www.amazon.com/gp/product/1430242337/ref=as_li_tl?ie=UTF8&camp=1789&creative=9325&creativeASIN=1430242337&linkCode=as2&tag=wiimp3-20&linkId=4ZT3NAHR7FYUMWWV

NinjaScript Reference

I'd also like to provide the link for the alphabetical NinjaScript language reference[a] - essential for NinjaScript development.

[a]http://www.ninjatrader.com/support/helpGuides/nt7/index.html?alphabetical_reference.htm

In the `Initialize` method, you'll notice we're utilizing the SetStopLoss[14] and SetProfitTarget[15] methods to set a stop loss and profit target for all of our trades - notice that we do not need to set this for each trade (although we could if necessary). It's important to note that `SetStopLoss` and `SetProfitTarget` in Percent mode both take double values as parameters. This means that .1 = 10%, .2 = 20%, etc.

In lines 15-16 of the `OnBarUpdate` method, we're making use of the NinjaScript SMA function[16] to get the 10 period and 20 period SMA (slightly different periods than in the etfdb.com article). The SMA method, as many NinjaScript indicators, returns an array of doubles - with the first array item being the most recent value and each subsequent value being one bar further in the past.

Once we have the values of the two indicators we're using in our strategy, we're making use of the NinjaScript CrossAbove method[17] which determines if one value has crossed from below to above a second value. In this line:

```
if (CrossAbove(sma10, sma20, 1))
```

We're going to enter the `if` statement if the 10 period SMA has crossed above the 20 period SMA within the previous bar (hence the "1"). This is the "Golden Cross" that our strategy is looking for.

And after this, our code is pretty self-documenting. Since we've met our condition, we're going to use the `EnterLong` to enter into a long position. Our strategy is very basic, and does not involve much logic for when to exit our position. The only time that we'll actually get out will be if the stop loss or profit target are hit.

[14]http://www.ninjatrader.com/support/helpGuides/nt7/setstoploss.htm

[15]http://www.ninjatrader.com/support/helpGuides/nt7/index.html?setprofittarget.htm

[16]http://www.ninjatrader.com/support/helpGuides/nt7/moving_average___simple_sma.htm

[17]http://www.ninjatrader.com/support/helpGuides/nt7/crossabove.htm

Compiling

Now that we have the strategy written, you can hit **F5** to compile the class for execution in the trading engine. Remember that you *cannot* run a strategy until it has been compiled. If you make updates in code, but forget to compile, you'll end up executing against the previously-compiled version of your code.

If there are compilation / syntax errors, you will see them at the bottom of the editor as shown below:

```
45      protected override void OnBarUpdate()
46      {
47          var sma10 = SMA(10);
48          var sma20 = SMA(20);
49
50          if (CrossAbove(sma10, sma20, 1)) {
51              EnterLong()
52          }
53      }
54
55      #region Properties
```

The following NinjaScript file(s) have programming errors and must be resolved before compiling:

NinjaScript File	Error	Code	Line
Strategy\DemoCrossoverSt	The name 'sma50' does not	CS0103 - click for info	46
Strategy\DemoCrossoverSt	; expected.		51
Strategy\DemoCrossoverSt	; expected	CS1002 - click for info	51

Image 'Compilation Exception'

After editing any errors, you should be able to re-compile until all messages have disappeared, at which point your strategy is ready for execution.

Summary

In this chapter, we've sketched out logic for a basic "Golden Cross" strategy and learned how to implement and compile it in NinjaScript (C#). Now that we have our strategy code written and compiled, in the next chapter, we'll see how to back-test this strategy against real historical data.

Chapter 4 : Strategy Backtesting

Introduction

Now for the fun stuff, seeing the (simulated) results of our work. In chapter 1 and chapter 2, we discussed automated trading basics, how to get NinjaTrader installed, and the auto-generation of a strategy class. In chapter 3, we dove into strategy code by implementing a basic Golden Cross strategy in C# code, and now, we'll demonstrate how to backtest that strategy using historical stock data to see how it would have performed in the real market.

Market Data

Before we get started, I'd like to point out that a very important part of backtesting, forward testing, optimization or live trade execution is getting good market data to utilize in your strategies. With the free version of NinjaTrader, the NinjaTrader partner Kinetick[18] provides a free data feed with end of day data - meaning that we can backtest daily bars for free. As you'll see on their site, Kinetick also sells (affordable) subscriptions to nearly any type of market data you'd like to consume in your trading strategy. You can confirm that you are connected to the Kinetic free end of day feed in the NinjaTrader menu shown below:

---

[18]http://www.kinetick.com/

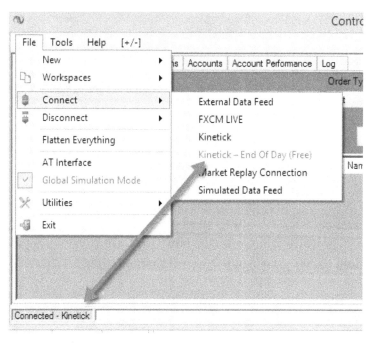

Connecting to Kinetick Free Data Feed

Strategy Analyzer - Backtesting

Once we've confirmed that we are connected to our data provider, let's start up a new strategy testing session by selecting the File⇒New⇒Strategy Analyzer menu item:

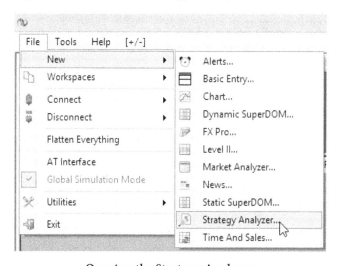

Opening the Strategy Analyzer

This will open a new strategy analyzer window which will function as a sandbox for our backtesting. In this open window, you'll see a tree-view in the left pane with a some default stock groups. For our first backtesting endeavor, let's try backtesting our Crossover strategy with Apple data for the past 2 years. As you might know, Apple is traded in the Nasdaq under symbol AAPL. Expand the

NASDAQ 100 node, select AAPL, right-click, and select "Backtest" as shown below (or alternatively click CTRL-B):

Backtest

If you're feeling particularly adventurous, you could even test the strategy against the entire NASDAQ 100 list - although the results become a little more difficult to interpret.

When you select this, a dock-able window will appear from the right side of the screen. Pin this to the screen using the Pin icon on the upper-right, select "DemoCrossoverStrategy" (or whatever you named your strategy) from the top drop-down and set the parameters as show below:

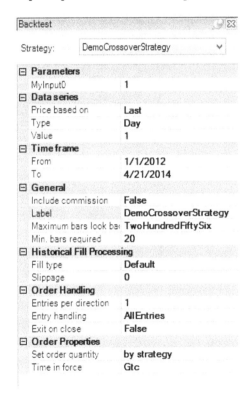

Backtesting Settings

Here are some highlights of the parameters we're setting here:

- **MyInput0**: This is the public property we mentioned in chapter 1. Although this value won't affect our strategy at all, this property will set the stage for the work we'll be doing in chapter 5 and chapter 6.
- **Data Series**: Here's where we set up our Bar size - and since we're using free end-of-day data, we'll set this to Day, 1.

- **Time frame:** This specifies the duration that we'll be backtesting. I'm going to go back to the beginning of 2012.
- **Exit on close:** Be sure to set this to "False", otherwise the orders we enter into won't be held over a night.
- **Include Commission:** In our example, we're not including the commission that would be charged to perform the trades. That is a slightly more advanced topic that we will touch on later in this chapter.

After these values have been set, go ahead and click "Run Backtest" to kick things off. After a short time, you should see results showing up in the Summary tab in the center pane.

Summary	Chart	Graphs	Executions	Trades	Periods	Orders	Settir

Performance	All Trades
Total Net Profit	$14102.00
Gross Profit	$38683.00
Gross Loss	$-24581.00
Commission	$0.00
Profit Factor	1.57
Cumulative Profit	30.08%
Max. Drawdown	-35.64%
Sharpe Ratio	0.05
Start Date	1/1/2011
End Date	4/21/2014
Total # of Trades	10
Percent Profitable	50.00%
# of Winning Trades	5
# of Losing Trades	5

Backtest Grid

As you can see, our strategy was overall profitable during this time period (see "Total Net Profit"), executing 10 trades, 5 of which were profitable. Take this success with a grain of salt though, as there are many factors that should be considered when evaluating whether a strategy will be successful when run against live data (hindsight is 20/20, right?). For more information on the data that is displayed in this grid, see this NinjaTrader page[19] for documentation.

Clicking on the Graph tab, we can see a visual representation of how the strategy's trades performed over time:

---

[19]http://www.ninjatrader.com/support/helpGuides/nt7/index.html?statistics_definitions.htm

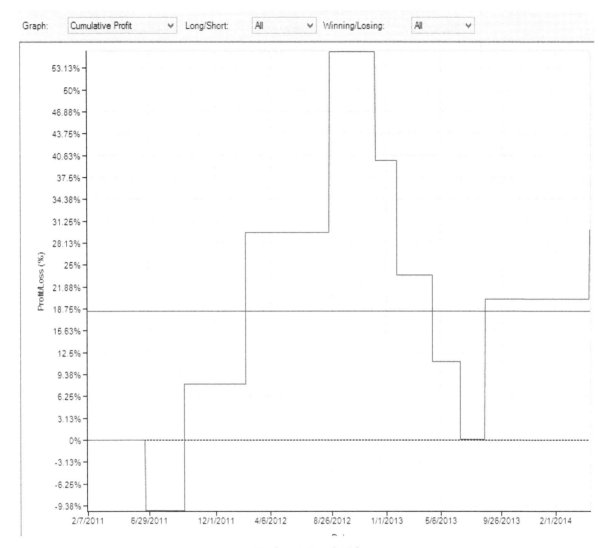

Backtest Graph Tab

And by clicking "Trades" we can see the details of each trade that was executed:

Tra	Quantity	Entry pric	Exit pric	Entry time	Exit time	Ent	Exit nam	Profit	Cum. pro
1	100	347.89	313.1	2/7/2011 3:00:00 PM	6/20/2011 3:00:00 PM	Bu	Stop los	-10.00 %	-10.00 %
2	100	343	411.6	7/5/2011 3:00:00 PM	9/19/2011 3:00:00 PM	Bu	Profit ta	20.00 %	8.00 %
3	100	401.35	481.62	10/19/2011 3:00:00 PM	2/9/2012 3:00:00 PM	Bu	Profit ta	20.00 %	29.60 %
4	100	561.5	673.8	6/4/2012 3:00:00 PM	8/21/2012 3:00:00 PM	Bu	Profit ta	20.00 %	55.52 %
5	100	586.79	528.11	11/30/2012 3:00:00 PM	12/6/2012 3:00:00 PM	Bu	Stop los	-10.00 %	39.97 %
6	100	521	460	1/11/2013 3:00:00 PM	1/24/2013 3:00:00 PM	Bu	Stop los	-11.71 %	23.58 %
7	100	457.69	411.92	2/20/2013 3:00:00 PM	4/17/2013 3:00:00 PM	Bu	Stop los	-10.00 %	11.22 %
8	100	455.71	410.14	5/6/2013 3:00:00 PM	6/21/2013 3:00:00 PM	Bu	Stop los	-10.00 %	0.10 %
9	100	425.01	510.01	7/15/2013 3:00:00 PM	8/19/2013 3:00:00 PM	Bu	Profit ta	20.00 %	20.12 %
10	100	490.51	531.17	10/3/2013 3:00:00 PM	4/21/2014 3:00:00 PM	Bu	Exit on	8.29 %	30.08 %

Backtest Trades Tab

Using these tools, we can pretty thoroughly evaluate how well our strategy would have done had it been executed during a past time period - amazingly powerful.

Now, let's say you want to make a tweak to your strategy and see the results - it can be done by:

1. Jump back into the NinjaScript Editor (or go to the Tools⇒Edit NinjaScript⇒Strategy menu from Control Center)
2. Make the desired change
3. Re-compile with an F5
4. Come back to the Strategy Analyzer
5. Right-click on a stock symbol ⇒ Backtest

Commission Fees

As you're probably very familiar with, real brokerages charge a fee for every trade you perform on the market. These fees can range across the board, depending on the broker and type of trade. In NinjaTrader, we can set these values in our options to have them automatically factored into the trading costs and backtested results, which can dramatically alter our results depending on the trade-frequency of the strategy.

To set a standard per-trade commission fee for your testing, start by going to Tools⇒Options in the main NinjaTrader menu. Once in the options menu, select "Commission", then scroll down to the "Stocks - Simulator" row as shown in the following screen shot:

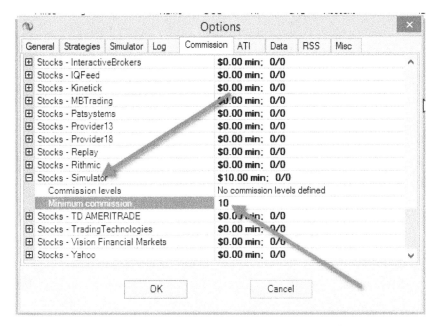

Commission Setting

Expanding this row will expose a "Minimum Commission" row, which you can set if you have a standard commission you'd like to set for all trades. If your brokerage offers a sliding scale for commission fees, it's also possible to set this up in the "Commission Levels" row - more information on custom levels is available here[20].

Once you have a Commission rate set, try running the same backtest and compare the result - possibly much less lucrative once we have to pay out money to a broker.

Summary

In this chapter, we've used the strategy we've created to perform a backtest, which executes our strategy logic against real historical data. This execution provided very good results, which we can use as a basis to predict the success of our strategy in future markets. In the next chapter, we'll learn how to use strategy optimization to optimize constant variable values for optimum results.

---

[20]http://www.ninjatrader.com/support/helpGuides/nt7/index.html?commission_tab.htm

Chapter 5 : Strategy Properties and Optimization

Introduction

In the previous chapters, we've covered some very interesting topics which have gotten us to the point of an automated strategy which we can backtest against historical data to see theoretical results. This type of testing is great if we already have a very specific strategy in mind with few variables or that have very well-specified values. If, however, we are devising a strategy that should work generally, but may need to be optimized specifically for a certain stock or market condition, then we can make use of NinjaTrader's strategy optimization features which allow us to define Strategy properties which the NinjaTrader backtester will supply with a range of values to determine what the best constant values might be. In this chapter, we'll do just that - adding public properties to our strategy, and then utilizing those properties to run optimizations.

Adding Strategy Properties

The first step in taking advantage of the NinjaTrader optimizer is to add public properties to the Strategy as we touched on in Chapter 2. Adding public properties allows us to expose pieces of our Strategy to the NinjaTrader backtester for potential optimization. To see how these properties can be utilized, let's start by adding 4 properties to our Strategy class, along with backing fields which will store their values.

In our Strategy, there are several values that we currently have hard-coded:

- The stop loss percentage
- The profit target percentage
- The low SMA value
- The high SMA value

These values are **perfect** candidates for optimization, since they are relatively arbitrary and may not be the best-possible for the tested equity / time period.

First, let's modify the *Variables* region in our class, removing the *private int myInput0 = 1;* variable that was auto-generated by NinjaTrader and adding 4 new field variables for the values we described above:

```
1   #region Variables
2   private int sma1Val = 10;
3   private int sma2Val = 20;
4   private int profitTarget = 10;
5   private int stopLoss = 20;
6   #endregion
```

Here you'll see that, in addition to creating the variables, I've also initialized them with "default" values. As we'll see momentarily, these values will show up in the NinjaTrader backtester as the default values for our strategy. Next, let's create the public properties to expose these fields:

```
1   #region Properties
2   [Description("First SMA Value")]
3   [GridCategory("Parameters")]
4   public int SMA1
5   {
6       get { return sma1Val; }
7       set { sma1Val = Math.Max(1, value); }
8   }
9
10  [Description("Second SMA Value")]
11  [GridCategory("Parameters")]
12  public int SMA2
13  {
14      get { return sma2Val; }
15      set { sma2Val = Math.Max(1, value); }
16  }
17
18  [Description("Stop Loss %")]
19  [GridCategory("Parameters")]
20  public int StopLoss
21  {
22      get { return stopLoss; }
23      set { stopLoss = Math.Max(1, value); }
24  }
25
26  [Description("Profit Target %")]
27  [GridCategory("Parameters")]
28  public int ProfitTarget
29  {
30      get { return profitTarget; }
31      set { profitTarget = Math.Max(1, value); }
```

```
32  }
33  #endregion
```

In this block, you'll notice a couple interesting things:

- We're adding a [GridCategory] attribute to each property. As you might guess, this value specifies the category of the property in the NinjaTrader backtester's grid. This value is *not* predetermined and can be set to any value that makes it easier for you to group properties.
- In the Setters, I'm using the Math.Max method to keep the set values greater than zero. This is not required, but is a handy way of doing validation (which is otherwise not possible).

Great, we now have properties with backing fields - now it's only necessary to update our Strategy's logic to utilize these new fields rather than the local variables we were using previously:

Modifying the Initialize method

```
1  protected override void Initialize()
2  {
3      CalculateOnBarClose = true;
4
5          // we'll set the stop loss for our positions globally
6          SetStopLoss(CalculationMode.Percent, Convert.ToDouble(this.stopLoss) / 100); // \
7  Stop Loss value set from 0.0 - 1.0
8              SetProfitTarget(CalculationMode.Percent, Convert.ToDouble(this.profitTarget) /\
9  100); // Profit Target value set from 0.0 - 1.0
10  }
```

Modifying the OnBarUpdate method

```
1  protected override void OnBarUpdate()
2  {
3          var sma1 = SMA(this.sma1Val);
4          var sma2 = SMA(this.sma2Val);
5
6          if (CrossAbove(sma1, sma2, 1)) {
7                  EnterLong();
8          }
9  }
```

Get the Code *Here's the link[21] to the Golden Cross strategy with our new Parameters.*

---

[21]https://gist.github.com/rymoore99/79c3b146b186206d200c

Strategy Analyzer - Optimizer

And, after re-compiling (F5) the Strategy, we can open up the NinaTrader Strategy Analyzer to see our new properties showing up.

Backtest

Strategy: DemoCrossoverStrategy2

SMA Parameters	
SMA1	10
SMA2	20
Target Parameters	
ProfitTarget	10
StopLoss	20

New Strategy Parameters - Backtest

With these properties now displaying in the Strategy Analyzer, you can easily try out different values by just changing the numbers in the property grid and re-running a backtest. As you'll see in the following figure, just a small change in these parameters can lead to very different results.

Summary	Chart	Graphs	Executions	Trades	Periods	Orders	Settings
Performance	All Trades	Long Trades	Short Trades	^
Total Net Profit	$-9164.00	$-9164.00	$0.00
Gross Profit	$7966.00	$7966.00	$0.00
Gross Loss	$-17130.00	$-17130.00	$0.00
Commission	$0.00	$0.00	$0.00
Profit Factor	0.47	0.47	1.00
Cumulative Profit	-17.65%	-17.65%	0.00%
Max. Drawdown	-30.00%	-30.00%	0.00%
Sharpe Ratio	1.00	1.00	1.00
Start Date	1/1/2012		
End Date	4/21/2014		
Total # of Trades	2	2	0
Percent Profitabl	50.00%	50.00%	0.00%
# of Winning Tra	1	1	0
# of Losing Trad	1	1	0

Backtest

Strategy: DemoCrossoverStrategy2

SMA Parameters	
SMA1	15
SMA2	40
Target r...	
ProfitTarget	30
StopLoss	30
Data series	
Price based on	Last
Type	Day
Value	1
Time frame	
From	1/1/2012
To	4/21/2014
General	
Include commission	False
Label	DemoCrossoverStrateg
Maximum bars look ba	TwoHundredFiftySix
Min. bars required	20

Very Different Results! - Backtest

With just a couple small tweaks to our thresholds, we've now gone from a strategy that looks like a sure-fire winner to a real dog. So how can we determine what the "best" values are for these properties? This is where optimization comes in, of course.

To get started optimizing, go back to the symbol list on the left-hand side of the screen, right-click on your symbol (AAPL) and this time, select Optimize (or CTRL-O).

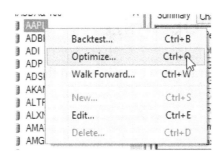

Selecting Optimize - Optimize

You'll now see a panel very similar to the Backtest properties panel.

Optimize	
Strategy:	DemoCrossoverStrategy2 ∨
SMA Parameters	
SMA1	10;10;1
Min. value	10
Max. value	10
Increment	1
SMA2	20;20;1
Target Parameters	
ProfitTarget	10;10;1
StopLoss	20;20;1
Min. value	20
Max. value	20
Increment	1
Optimize	
Keep best # results	10
Optimize data series	False
Optimize on...	max. profit factor
Optimizer	Default

New Strategy Parameters - Optimize

Our properties in the property grid now have become a bit more complex, containing a "Min Value", "Max Value", and an "Increment". Using these properties, we're now able to specify a range of values that will be tested to find a "sweet spot" for strategy success.

Optimization Times and Property Ranges

Optimization takes time! The wider the range between the Min and Max, along with the size of the Increment value will make for longer times to optimize your results, especially if you're optimizing many input variables. Depending on your strategy, it may be best to start with a wide Min/Max range, but a high increment to get a general feel for the results, then fine-tune with a tighter range of values.

In our Strategy, we have 4 properties that can be optimized. Let's now add a range for each of these values and use the default optimization properties (which we'll discuss in a moment) to run an optimization.

SMA Parameters	
SMA1	10;20;2
Min. value	10
Max. value	20
Increment	2
SMA2	20;40;5
Min. value	20
Max. value	40
Increment	5
Target Parameters	
ProfitTarget	5;20;5
Min. value	5
Max. value	20
Increment	5
StopLoss	5;20;5
Min. value	5
Max. value	20
Increment	5

Setting Property Ranges - Optimize

And, by clicking "Run Optimization", the NinjaTrader optimizer kicks off, running a backtest for *every possible* combination of the properties. Depending on the range and number of increments we've specified, this can take quite a while - and as you'll notice, the Strategy Optimizer window only shows "Optmization in Progress". To get a good estimate of the actual time left in the optimization, you'll need to jump back to the Control Center window as shown in the following screen shot:

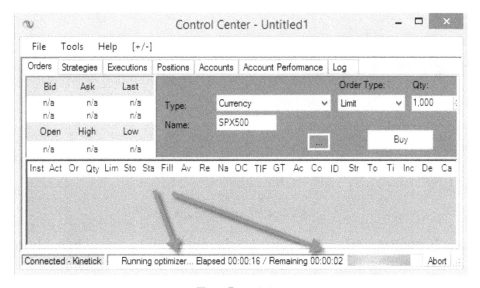

Time Remaining

And after an optimization, we get a grid showing the *best* result based on the "Optimize on..." property we've selected.

Instrument	Performance	Total Net P ▽	Gross Profit	Gross Loss	Profit Factor	Cumulative P	Max. Drawdo	Total # of Tra	Percent Profita
AAPL	99	$21,304.00	$21,304.00	$0.00	99.00	46.08 %	0.00 %	3	100.00 %

Summary | Chart | Graphs | Executions | Trades | Periods | Orders | Settings

Performance	All Trades	Long Trades	Short Trades
Total Net Profit	$21304.00	$21304.00	$0.00
Gross Profit	$21304.00	$21304.00	$0.00
Gross Loss	$0.00	$0.00	$0.00
Commission	$0.00	$0.00	$0.00
Profit Factor	99.00	99.00	1.00
Cumulative Profit	46.08%	46.08%	0.00%
Max. Drawdown	0.00%	0.00%	0.00%
Sharpe Ratio	39430.21	39430.21	1.00
Start Date	1/1/2012		
End Date	4/21/2014		
Total # of Trades	3	3	0
Percent Profitable	100.00%	100.00%	0.00%
# of Winning Trades	3	3	0
# of Losing Trades	0	0	0

All Optimization Results

By selecting the "Optimizer" tab, we can also see the results of the top 10 property combinations, and the property values that were used to achieve these results (see the Parameters column).

Instrument	Performan	Parameters	Total Net Pro	Gross Profit	Gross Loss	Profit Factor	Cumulative P	Max. Drawdo	Total # of Tra	Percent Profitable
AAPL	99	20/10/40/20 (ProfitTarget/SMA1/SMA2/StopLoss)	$21,304.00	$21,304.00	$0.00	99.00	46.08 %	0.00 %	3	100.00 %
AAPL	99	15/10/40/20 (ProfitTarget/SMA1/SMA2/StopLoss)	$16,167.00	$16,167.00	$0.00	99.00	34.16 %	0.00 %	3	100.00 %
AAPL	99	10/10/40/20 (ProfitTarget/SMA1/SMA2/StopLoss)	$16,006.00	$16,006.00	$0.00	99.00	35.02 %	0.00 %	4	100.00 %
AAPL	99	5/10/40/20 (ProfitTarget/SMA1/SMA2/StopLoss)	$8,381.00	$8,381.00	$0.00	99.00	17.43 %	0.00 %	4	100.00 %
AAPL	99	15/10/35/20 (ProfitTarget/SMA1/SMA2/StopLoss)	$16,465.00	$16,465.00	$0.00	99.00	34.28 %	0.00 %	3	100.00 %
AAPL	99	10/10/35/20 (ProfitTarget/SMA1/SMA2/StopLoss)	$16,114.00	$16,114.00	$0.00	99.00	35.14 %	0.00 %	4	100.00 %
AAPL	99	5/10/35/20 (ProfitTarget/SMA1/SMA2/StopLoss)	$8,458.00	$8,458.00	$0.00	99.00	17.54 %	0.00 %	4	100.00 %
AAPL	5.11	15/10/40/5 (ProfitTarget/SMA1/SMA2/StopLoss)	$18,816.00	$23,393.00	-$4,577.00	5.11	39.24 %	-9.75 %	6	66.67 %
AAPL	5.1	15/10/35/5 (ProfitTarget/SMA1/SMA2/StopLoss)	$18,788.00	$23,365.00	-$4,577.00	5.10	39.37 %	-9.75 %	6	66.67 %
AAPL	4.59	20/10/40/5 (ProfitTarget/SMA1/SMA2/StopLoss)	$16,412.00	$20,989.00	-$4,577.00	4.59	31.84 %	-9.75 %	5	60.00 %

Optimization Result Properties

As you can see in these results, our original parameters for SMA1, SMA2, profit target, and stop loss were not the most optimal. The "best" property values to optimize profit factor for AAPL in this timeframe were:

- SMA1: 10
- SMA2: 40
- ProfitTarget: 20
- Stop Loss: 20

Optimize On

When we're running a strategy optimization, a *very* important factor in determining "success" is how we are measuring results. An obvious answer would seem to be "Net Profit", but that's not always the case, as sometimes the most profitable strategies over a time period turn out to be exceptionally risky strategies in others. NinjaTrader provides a number of out-of-the-box optimization measures, and it's also possible to create custom classes to measure success.

Custom Optimization

We won't cover the custom creation in this book, but if you look at the classes found in [My Documents Directory]\NinjaTrader 7\bin\Custom\Type, you'll see all of the optimization options in the drop-down, and can add additional as you'd like.

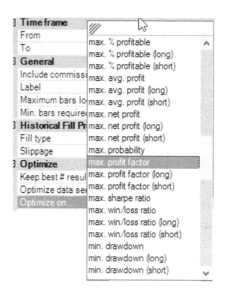

Optimize On Options

Listed below are some of the common optimization options:

- Max % Profitable: Maximizes the percentage of the strategy's trades that are profitable.
- Max net profit: Maximizes the total net profit of the strategy
- Max profit factor: Maximizes gross profit vs gross loss
- Max Sharpe ratio: Sharpe Ratio[22] is a measurement of strategy performance that also takes risk into its calculation.
- Max win/loss ratio: Maximizes the ratio of winning trades to losing trades
- Max drawdown: Gives a better score to strategies that don't require drawing into negative territory in your account balance (which everyone can appreciate).

A more detailed description of each of these optimization options is available at this link[23].

Genetic Optimization

We've mentioned a few times here about how long an optimization can possibly take - well, if there is a range of values you **really** want to try, but don't want to wait for **every** combination to get tested, NinjaTrader also has the option for a Genetic Optimization which will use a genetic algorithm[24] similar to that used in biology's version of natural selection which can test out a subset of possible values and (hopefully) find something close to the optimal result. Depending on the settings you choose, the genetic optimization should take significantly less time than a full optimization.

[22]http://www.investopedia.com/terms/s/sharperatio.asp

[23]http://www.ninjatrader.com/support/helpGuides/nt7/index.html?statistics_definitions.htm

[24]http://en.wikipedia.org/wiki/Genetic_algorithm

Important Note

Just be sure to understand that when you're doing a Genetic optimization, you're not getting the absolutely best result obtained by doing an exhaustive search, but instead a "very good" result (which *could* be the absolute best) in less time.

To use the genetic optimization, select "Genetic" from the "Optimizer" property, as shown in the following screen shot:

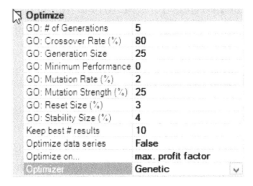

Optimize

GO: # of Generations	5
GO: Crossover Rate (%)	80
GO: Generation Size	25
GO: Minimum Performance	0
GO: Mutation Rate (%)	2
GO: Mutation Strength (%)	25
GO: Reset Size (%)	3
GO: Stability Size (%)	4
Keep best # results	10
Optimize data series	False
Optimize on...	max. profit factor
Optimizer	Genetic

Optimize On Options

For a full description of all of the genetic optimization properties, see the NinjaTrader documentation[25].

Summary

In this chapter, we've shown how to extend our class with public properties and then optimize our strategy properties using the NinjaTrader optimizer. This can be a *huge* help in determining potential strategy viability, but, as with backtesting, should be interpreted with a grain of salt, since it's performed exclusively on historical data, which can possibly result in strategies that work amazingly well in the past, but not at all in the future.

---

[25]http://www.ninjatrader.com/support/helpGuides/nt7/index.html?genetic_algorithm.htm

Chapter 6 : Strategy Debugging

Introduction

In chapter 2 & chapter 3, we covered some basic strategy development which can help get you started in many scenarios. Unfortunately, strategy development can often be difficult and not all development goes as planned the first time through. To help troubleshoot the development process, in this chapter, we'll cover two methods of strategy debugging - Logging and Visual Studio debugging.

NinjaScript Print Method

If you've ever worked with a .NET console application, you're probably very familiar with the *Console.WriteLine* method which allows you to shoot messages to the console output. One of the easiest methods of debugging a NinjaScript strategy is to utilize a very similar NinjaScript method, Print[26]. With the `Print` method, you can send text to the NinjaTrader Output window which can contain information about the current state of your application which should assist in debugging and troubleshooting.

To get a feel for the simple `Print` statement, let's modify our Strategy, adding a `Print` output any time we enter a position, as in the following code block:

Adding Logging to the OnBarUpdate method

```
1  protected override void OnBarUpdate()
2  {
3          var sma1 = SMA(sma1Val);
4          var sma2 = SMA(sma2Val);
5
6          if (CrossAbove(sma1, sma2, 1)) {
7                  EnterLong();
8
9                  var msg = string.Format("Entering long. SMA1={0}, SMA2={1}, Price={2}",
10                         sma1[0], sma2[0], Close[0]);
11                 Print(msg);
12         }
13 }
```

---

[26]http://www.ninjatrader.com/support/helpGuides/nt7/index.html?print.htm

Pretty simple, right? After re-compiling, let's go back into the NinjaTrader Strategy Analyzer and run a backtest on the Strategy to see the output (Print does work with optimizations as well).

In order to view the Print results, it's necessary to open up the Output window in the Analyzer by clicking on the Output toolbar icon, as shown in the following screenshot.

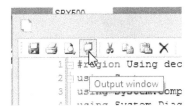

Opening Output Window - Backtest

And now, after kicking off the backtest, we'll see our Print messages spit out on the Output screen.

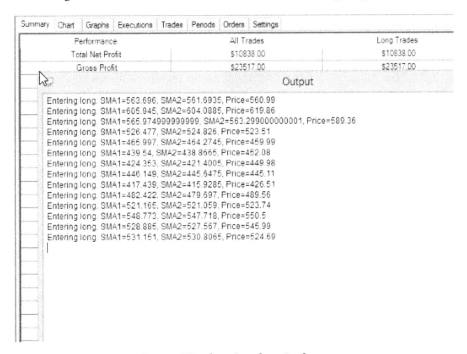

Output Window Results - Backtest

NinjaScript ClearOutputWindow Method

This works great, but one thing you'll find is that, after running multiple backtests or optimizations, the output results begin to blend together, making it very hard to determine when one backtest session started and the next begins. Fortunately, NinjaScript contains a helper method, ClearOutputWindow[27], which we can use to clear the contents of the output window before a test run.

To finish up our Print test, let's add a call to this method in the Initialize method of our Strategy, which will clear out the Output window before each backtest execution.

---

[27] http://www.ninjatrader.com/support/helpGuides/nt7/index.html?clearoutputwindow.htm

Adding ClearOutputWindow to the Initialize method

```
1
2  {   protected override void Initialize()
3
4          ClearOutputWindow();
5
6  }         ...
```

Although it is a very simple method compared to the Visual Studio debugging that .NET developers have become used to, the Print method can be a great tool for debugging or monitoring your strategy backtests and optimizations.

Get the Code *Here's the link[28] to the newly modified code we've created for reference.*

Strategy Debugging with Visual Studio

Strategy debugging in Visual Studio is one of those somewhat undocumented features that *really* makes life a lot easier. Unfortunately, there are a few quirks to overcome to effectively do VS debugging, but once you get used to them, it's a breeze!

Visual Studio Express

In case you don't have Visual Studio, I'd recommend downloading and installing Visual Studio 2012 Express, available at:

http://www.microsoft.com/en-us/download/details.aspx?id=34673[29]

This free version of Visual Studio will work perfectly for strategy debugging.

Attaching to the NinjaTrader Process

Once you have Visual Studio up and running, here are the steps necessary to attach to a Strategy Analyzer session and begin debugging our Golden Cross strategy:

1. Open Visual Studio
2. Go to File ⇒ Open ⇒ File (or ctrl-O)
3. Navigate to [your documents folder]NinjaTrader 7\binCustomStrategy (for example: c:\administrator\documentsNinjaTrader 7\binCustomStrategy\ as mentioned at the end of Chapter 2)

---

[28]https://gist.github.com/rymoore99/64c429317bdf43598fd0

[29]http://www.microsoft.com/en-us/download/details.aspx?id=34673

4. Select the file name of the Strategy you've created
5. Go to Debug ⇒ Attach to Process menu and choose the NinjaTrader process as shown below:

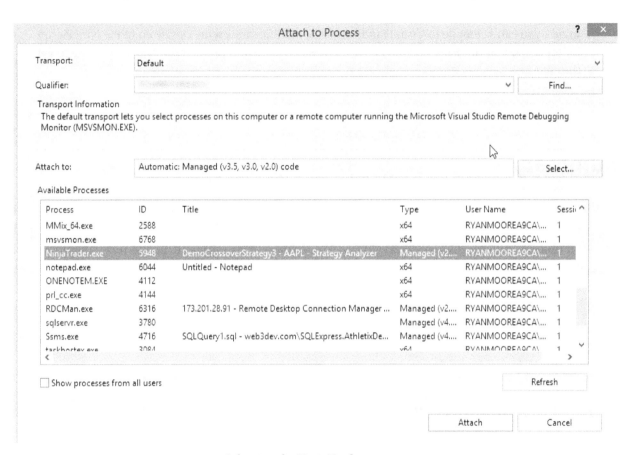

Selecting the NinjaTrader process

1. Put a breakpoint in your code.
2. Go back to NinjaTrader and run a backtest

You'll see that your breakpoint will get hit, as shown in in the following screenshot, which will allow you to view variable values, etc, just like you can in any other .NET application!

```
protected override void OnBarUpdate()
{
    var sma1 = SMA(sma1Val);
    var sma2 = SMA(sma2Val);

    if (CrossAbove(sma1, sma2, 1)) {
        EnterLong();     ⊞ ● sma1 {SMA(AAPL (Daily),10)} ▣
        var msg = string.Format("Entering long. SMA1={0}, SMA2={1}, Price={2}", sma1[0], sma2[0], Close[0]);
        Print(msg);
    }
}
```

Output Window - Backtest

> **Note**
>
> You can make edits to your strategy file in Visual Studio (or any other external editor) but keep in mind - you can't compile in Visual Studio and the modifications **won't** show up in the NinjaScript Editor when you flip back to compile. You'll need to close and re-open the NinjaScript file to get the changes!

Summary

In this chapter, we've covered the basics of NinjaScript strategy debugging using the Print method and the Visual Studio IDE. Each of these tools will come in handy in different circumstances, and the combination will be invaluable as you tackle strategy development! In the next chapter, we'll look at the more advanced topic of database connectivity from within a NinjaScript strategy class.

Chapter 7 : Database Connectivity

Introduction

In the previous chapters, we've covered many relatively basic topics, ranging from simple strategy creation to Visual Studio debugging. While these skills will suffice for much strategy development, for more complex strategies it may be very useful to connect to a database in order to record results or run queries to determine logic. In this chapter, we're going to modify our GoldenCross strategy to log to a SQL Server database, which will provide a foundation for any database connectivity your strategy may require.

Setting up SQL Express

As an example of database connectivity, we're going to modify our existing strategy to log info and errors to a Microsoft SQL Express database. Being able to do INSERTs should provide a good reference for any SQL database operations you may want to do (SELECTing Tweets from a Twitter table, UPDATEing strategy trades in a StrategyTradeLog table, etc). If you don't already have SQL Express or another version of SQL Server installed, you can download it from:

http://www.microsoft.com/en-us/download/details.aspx?id=29062[30]

The default setup should work fine for our logging example - I have chosen to use Windows Authentication rather than SQL Server authentication, but either should work just fine.

Once you have SQL Server set up, fire up either Visual Studio or SQL Server Management Tool to create a new database. I won't walk through the specifics of database creation (although it's very easy), but I have created a new DB called "NinjaTest1" with a single "Log" table with schema as defined below:

---

[30]http://www.microsoft.com/en-us/download/details.aspx?id=29062

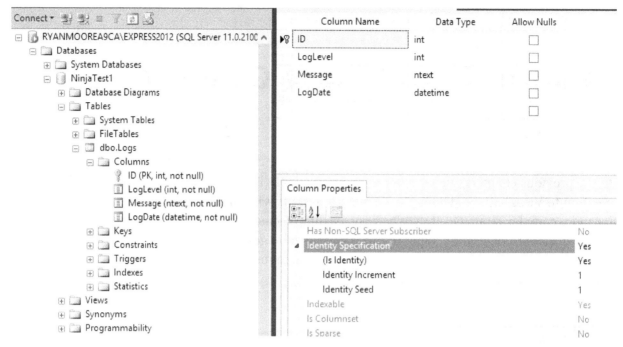

NinjaTest1 Schema

With this table created, we're ready to move back into the NinjaScript editor.

Adding a DLL Reference

As you've probably gathered at this point, your NinjaScript file has access to many of the assemblies in the .NET Framework, as is obvious by the using declarations already in the top of our strategy file:

```
1   using System;
2   using System.ComponentModel;
3   using System.Diagnostics;
4   using System.Drawing;
5   using System.Drawing.Drawing2D;
6   using System.Xml.Serialization;
```

The default list of .NET assemblies however, does not include System.Data, which is necessary to connect to SQL Server. In order to make our SQL connection, we first need to add a reference to System.Data.dll.

IMPORTANT - .NET Version

NinjaTrader is compiled against the .NET 3.5 framework, so any references MUST be made against the .NET 2.0 or 3.5 assemblies *NOT* the 4.0+ assemblies.

Probably the easiest way to get the .NET 2.0 System.Data.dll is to:

1. Create a new Console application in Visual Studio.
2. Change it to compile for the .NET 2.0 framework as shown below:

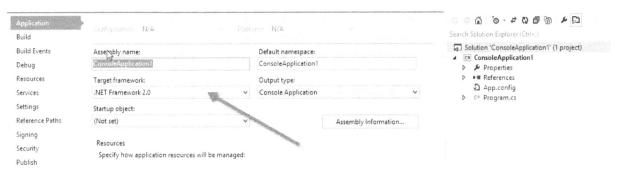

Compiling for .NET 2.0

1. Add System.Data.dll to the references

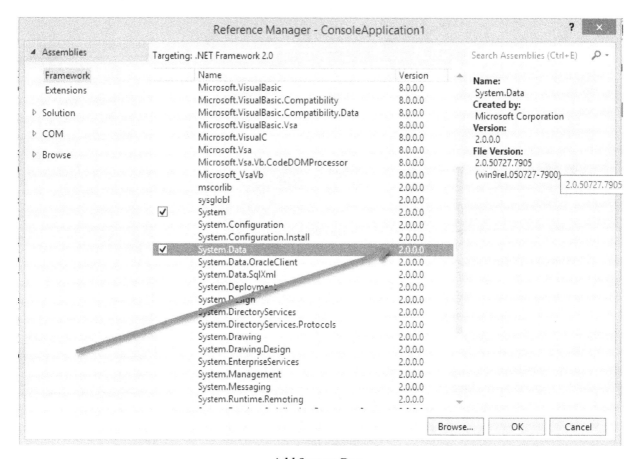

Add System.Data

1. Right Click on System.Data in the references, select "Properties", and change "Copy Local" to True

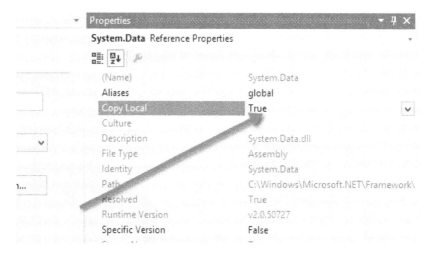

Add System.Data

1. Compile the application and go to the bin\debug folder.
2. Grab the System.Data.dll file!

OR... I have extracted this file and have it available for direct download at this link:

https://dl.dropboxusercontent.com/u/14382853/ninja/System.Data.dll[31]

Once you have System.Data.dll available, we'll need to copy it into a location where NinjaTrader can access it. This location is:

[My Documents]NinjaTrader 7\binCustom

Name	Date modified	Type	Size
ExportNinjaScript	4/16/2014 3:01 PM	File folder	
Indicator	1/25/2014 5:54 AM	File folder	
MarketAnalyzer	1/25/2014 5:54 AM	File folder	
Strategy	6/11/2014 2:35 PM	File folder	
Tmp	6/11/2014 2:22 PM	File folder	
Type	1/25/2014 5:53 AM	File folder	
._.DS_Store	4/16/2014 3:00 PM	DS_STORE File	4 KB
.DS_Store	4/16/2014 3:00 PM	DS_STORE File	7 KB
AssemblyInfo.cs	1/14/2014 5:15 AM	CS File	1 KB
NinjaTrader.Custom.csproj	4/23/2012 1:34 AM	CSPROJ File	20 KB
NinjaTrader.Custom.dll	6/11/2014 5:44 AM	Application extens...	400 KB
NinjaTrader.Custom.xml	6/11/2014 5:44 AM	XML File	469 KB
NinjaTrader.Vendor.cs	4/23/2012 1:33 AM	CS File	26 KB
NinjaTrader.Vendor.dll	1/14/2014 1:30 PM	Application extens...	65 KB
System.Data.dll	7/9/2012 1:40 AM	Application extens...	1,137 KB

This PC ▸ Documents ▸ NinjaTrader 7 ▸ bin ▸ Custom ▸   ∨ ⟳   Search Custom

Once you have the .dll in the 'Custom' folder, we're finally ready to add a reference.

Back in the NinjaScript editor, right-click anywhere in the window and select "References".

[31]https://dl.dropboxusercontent.com/u/14382853/ninja/System.Data.dll

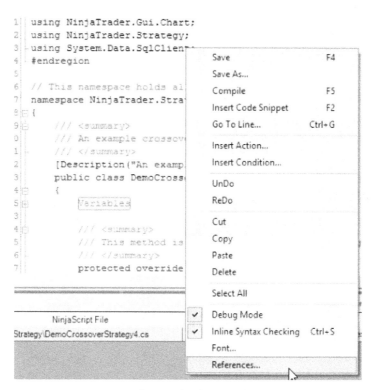

Selecting 'References'

In the following window, click "Add" and select the System.Data.dll that you've just copied to the Custom directory.

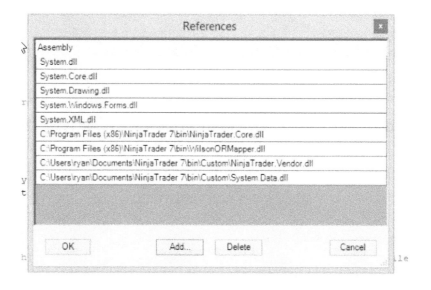

And with that, we now have the correct reference to System.Data.

Connecting to the Database

Now that we've covered the setup work necessary to utilize the System.Data .dll, we'll (finally) start adding code to our NinjaScript strategy. The first step will be to reference the System.Data.SqlClient namespace in the 'Using declarations' region as shown below

Adding System.Data.SqlClient

```
#region Using declarations
using System;
...
using System.Data.SqlClient;
#endregion
```

And, with the namespace available, we'll create a new, class-level field called connection, which we will initialize in the Initialize method with a SQL connection string. Notice that I've left out the server details which you will need to replace with your own custom server name.

Once we have the connection initialized, we'll open it up within a try-catch block, as shown in lines 53-58.

Adding System.Data.SqlClient and initializing Connection

```
39  public class DemoCrossoverStrategy4 : Strategy
40  {
41          private SqlConnection connection;
42
43          ...
44
45          protected override void Initialize()
46      {
47                  ClearOutputWindow();
48
49          CalculateOnBarClose = true;
50
51                  // we'll set the stop loss for our positions globally
52                  SetStopLoss(CalculationMode.Percent, Convert.ToDouble(stopLoss) / 100);
53                      SetProfitTarget(CalculationMode.Percent, Convert.ToDouble(profitTarget) / 100\
54  );
55
56                  connection = new SqlConnection("server=YOUR SERVER HERE;" +
57                              "Trusted_Connection=yes;" +
58                              "database=NinjaTest1; " +
```

```
59                                          "connection timeout=30");
60
61          try {
62                  this.connection.Open();
63                  }
64                  catch {
65                          Print("Error opening SQL Connection");
66                  }
67          }
```

Wow, big steps here! We've now added code to connect to our database. This connection gets opened up when the strategy comes into existence - and next, we need to add code to close the connection when the strategy is complete. To do this, we'll add code to the OnTermination method[32] which NinjaTrader.Strategy.Strategy allows us to override:

Closing the Database Connection

```
77  protected override void OnTermination()
78  {
79          if (this.connection != null)
80                  this.connection.Close();
81  }
```

At this point, we've created code that creates, opens, and closes a SQL connection - so the only thing left to do is add code that will insert records into our 'Logs' table when needed:

Adding Log Methods

```
83  private void LogInfo(string msg) {
84          LogToDB(1, msg);
85          Print("INFO: " + msg);
86  }
87
88  private void LogError(string msg) {
89          LogToDB(2, msg);
90          Print("ERROR: " + msg);
91  }
92
93  private void LogToDB(int logLevel, string msg) {
94          try
95      {
```

---

[32]http://www.ninjatrader.com/support/helpGuides/nt7/index.html?ontermination.htm

```
96                  var query = "INSERT INTO Logs (LogLevel, Message, LogDate) VALUES (@logLevel, @\
97  message, GETDATE())";
98                  using (var cmd = new SqlCommand(query, this.connection)) {
99                          cmd.Parameters.AddWithValue("@logLevel", logLevel);
100                         cmd.Parameters.AddWithValue("@message", msg);
101
102                         cmd.ExecuteNonQuery();
103                 }
104     }
105     catch (Exception e)
106     {
107                 Print("Error Logging to Database: " + e.ToString());
108     }
109 }
```

I won't dive into the specifics of the SqlCommand object used here, as there are many resources[33] available online, but hopefully these two methods are very straight-forward.

Lastly, we'll just need to add a call to our new LogInfo method in our OnBarUpdate method:

Adding Log call

```
64  protected override void OnBarUpdate()
65  {
66          var sma1 = SMA(sma1Val);
67          var sma2 = SMA(sma2Val);
68
69          if (CrossAbove(sma1, sma2, 1)) {
70                  EnterLong();
71
72                  var msg = string.Format("Entering long. SMA1={0}, SMA2={1}, Price={2}", sma1[0]\
73  , sma2[0], Close[0]);
74
75                  LogInfo(msg);
76          }
77  }
```

Get the Code *The full, newly modified strategy is available at this link*[34]

And with that, we should have log records being sent to the database. If you re-compile (F5), jump back to the Strategy Analyzer, and re-run a Backtest or Optimization, you should see Log records showing up in your database.

---

[33] https://www.google.com/search?q=sqlcommand+example&oq=sqlcommand+example&aqs=chrome..69i57j0l5.4234j0j7&sourceid=chrome&es_sm=91&ie=UTF-8#q=C%23%20sqlcommand%20example&safe=off

[34] https://gist.github.com/rymoore99/19e27eae333d61b8bd41

Summary

In this chapter, we've made some great jumps, learning how to add additional .dll references to a NinjaScript strategy, and then using that assembly to connect to a SQL Server database. Using very similar code, it would be possible to connect to a MySQL or Oracle database and query any amount of data before making trades. Hopefully this helps open some doors for great trades!

Next Steps

In this book, we've taken a whirl-wind spin through NinjaScript strategy development, covering topics ranging from basic NinjaTrader setup to more complex debugging and database connectivity. These skills should provide a great foundation to help get your trading strategy ideas off the ground, backtested, and into the real world.

Of course, there are many additional tools and topics that have not been covered in this brief introduction, including:

- Forward Testing
- Indicator Development
- Running with a real brokerage account against the live market

For more information on these and other topics, or to ask questions and participate in great discussions, please join this book's discussion forum at:

https://groups.google.com/forum/#!forum/automated-stock-trading-csharp[35]

And, for customized help in strategy development or C# training, please contact us at:

http://www.strategyminer.net[36]

Happy trading!

---

[35]https://groups.google.com/forum/#!forum/automated-stock-trading-csharp
[36]http://www.strategyminer.net

www.ingramcontent.com/pod-product-compliance
Lightning Source LLC
Chambersburg PA
CBHW082113070326
40689CB00052B/4658